How to Potty Train a Toddler

Potty Train Your Child without the Stress

Daniel Robinson

Liability Disclaimer

By reading this book, you assume all risks associated with using the advice given below, with a full understanding that you, solely, are responsible for anything that may occur as a result of putting this information into action in any way, and regardless of your interpretation of the advice.

You further agree that our company cannot be held responsible in any way for the success or failure of your business as a result of the information presented in this book. It is your responsibility to conduct your own due diligence regarding the safe and successful operation of your business if you intend to apply any of our information in any way to your business operations.

Terms of Use

You are given a non-transferable, "personal use" license to this book. You cannot distribute it or share it with other individuals.

Also, there are no resale rights or private label rights granted when purchasing this book. In other words, it's for your own personal use only.

How to Potty Train a Toddler

Potty Train Your Child without the Stress

Table of Contents

Introduction - What You Need to Know Before You Start 9

Chapter 1 - How to Know Your Child is Ready for Potty Training 11

Chapter 2 - Start Preparation Ahead of Time 15

Chapter 3 -Things You Need to Buy 17

Chapter 4 - How to Stop Stressing 21

Chapter 5 - Getting Started 23

Chapter 6 - Day One of Potty Training 25

Chapter 7 - Potty Training for Boys 29

Chapter 8 - Potty Training for Girls 31

Chapter 9 - Books and DVDs Can Help 33

Chapter 10 - Tricks and Games to Make Potty Training More Fun 35

Chapter 11 - 7 Things to Never Do When You are Potty Training Your Child 39

Chapter 12 - Overnight Potty Training 41

Chapter 13 - What to Do When You Travel 43

Chapter 14 – Possible Problems.....................................47

Conclusion 49

Introduction - What You Need to Know Before You Start

Toilet training your child can seem like a daunting task. It brings fear to the minds of many parents. It's almost as bad as teaching your child to drive; but not quite.

The main thing to remember before you start potty training is that your child will succeed. Maybe not in your time-line or as quickly as you'd prefer; but they will learn. You will not be sending your child to high school in diapers. This is just one step in a long line of things your child will master as they grow up.

In this guide will explain how to tell when your child is showing signs that they are ready to be potty trained. I'll also explain why it will be stressful if you try to start too soon.

As you start this new adventure make sure your spouse is on board with the potty training system you've chosen. You don't want to be pulling the child in two directions. You need to have a plan that you've discussed in advance and that you both understand and agree upon. Potty training requires consistency and everyone in the family needs to be involved.

Let's get started.

Chapter 1 - How to Know Your Child is Ready for Potty Training

One of the biggest reasons parents have a hard time with potty training is they start too soon. Not all children mature at the same rate. Even if you read a book that says to start training at 22 months doesn't mean that your child will be ready at that time.

Most children are ready sometime between 22 and 30 months. But those are only guidelines. A few are ready sooner, a few aren't ready until later. Don't expect your child to fall into anyone else's time line.

Don't listen to other mother's who tell you that their child was potty trained by the time they were one year old. What they're really saying is that they (the parent) were trained. They may have been able to get their child to the potty on time; but the child was not potty trained. Plus, they're probably exaggerating, anyway.

If your child is not yet ready don't let anyone make you feel guilty for waiting.

Here are the signs you need to look for to help you decide if your child is ready:

They need to be able to walk, stand, and sit on their own and be able to communicate using a few words or gestures.

Can they sit for at least five minutes at a time?

A big part of being ready for potty training is whether your child can control his bladder and bowel movements.

Some of the signs of this include:

- Are they going 2-4 hours with a dry diaper?

- Do they have regular bowel movements?

- Are they still having bowel movements at night?

- Do they tell you when they have a wet or messy diaper?

- Are they dry after napping for one or two hours?

- Some of the physical tasks the need to be able to do include:

- Can they take their pants on and off without help?

When they start asking to use the toilet or to wear "big kid" underwear then you'll know for sure it's time.

Sadly, due to preschool requirements some parents feel pressured to start potty training before their child is truly ready. If you have no choice but to start your child's training early then be prepared for it to take longer and to experience a few set-backs along the way.

If your child is still at the stage where they say "NO!" to everything; it can make potty training a real challenge for both of you. When you must start training when they're in this stage; do as much advance preparation as possible to set the stage and prepare them. Try to be as positive as you can and not let in turn into a battle of wills if possible.

Remember, it's important to start training when your child is ready; not when YOU are ready. Because of the high cost of diapers and problems such as diaper rash; parents are anxious for their children to be diaper free. But just because you are ready does not mean your child is ready. Watch for the signs and potty training will be much easier for both of you.

Chapter 2 - Start Preparation Ahead of Time

Make a plan. Deciding one day that you'll start potty training without any advance preparation is a recipe for disaster.

Take some time to make your plan, get all your supplies ready, and get your child prepared for his or her new adventure. Make sure everyone in the family understands how important this time will be for your child. This includes your spouse, the child's older siblings, and even care givers and baby-sitters.

Whenever you talk to your child about potty training act excited and happy.

There are several things you can do to prepare your home and your child for potty training. This will start to set the stage for successful training.

Let them watch the adults in the house use the restroom.

This helps them understand what is going on the bathroom.

Decide on the words you're going to use. Will you say "poop" and "wee wee" for a bowel movement and urinating? What do you want your son to call his penis? The words you use don't really matter as long as you're consistent and your child understands what you mean. Make sure your spouse and babysitters know the words you are using with your child, also.

Track your child's pattern as much as can. Write down when they have wet diapers and bowel movements. This will help you know if your child is ready for training and also when you'll need to be sure and have them on the potty.

Try not to start training when your family is going through a time of transition such as a divorce, moving to a new house, the birth of a new baby, or any other big household or family changes.

Pick a day when you're going to be home all day to get started. Put a big star on the calendar. Let your child know that this is an important day for them. But always do it in a fun way, not a way that makes them feel stressed or pressured.

Chapter 3 -Things You Need to Buy

Some parents choose to have their children potty train on a normal toilet. If you do this you will probably need a step stool so your child can reach the toilet on their own. But they will still need in the beginning.

There are pros and cons about using a potty chair. It's usually much easier for a child to use a potty chair without help. They are also sometimes willing to sit on a small chair longer because they don't feel like they're going to fall and it's more comfortable. Another advantage is your child can sit on "his" toilet while you're sitting on the big toilet. Being able to rest their feet firmly on the ground also helps them with bowel movements.

The cons are it's sometimes harder for the child to then use a regular toilet when you're at a public restroom or someone else's home. They'll be use to their potty but not comfortable on a regular size toilet.

Either option will work you'll just need to weigh the pros and cons for your situation.

If you're going to use a potty chair then that will be on the top of your "to buy" list. There are many models available now. You can even shop online if you want to explore a lot of options without ever leaving your house.

It can be a good idea to let your child help pick out their potty chair. Narrow your choices down to two or three options first. Then let them choose the one they want. It will give them a feeling of ownership. You might want to paint your child's name on the potty. Long before they can read they recognize their name and they'll know it's "their" special chair.

Pull up pants and underwear are another thing for your shopping list. You might want to let your child help pick these out, too. They'll love wearing underwear with cartoon characters if you choose to go that route. But once you start, it's then hard to get them wear "plain" underwear! It can be good incentive, though, to get them excited about the idea of wearing underwear.

Help them understand that wearing underwear is part of being a "big kid".

Buy some story books and DVDs about potty training. We'll talk about this again in Chapter Ten.

Rewards and prizes for successful days can be a big part of successful potty training . If you decide to use this method have the items purchased in advance.

Consider buying a doll that wets. This is a good way for

your child to understand the concept of potty training. They can practice pulling down the pants of the doll and sitting it on the potty chair. Then they'll see that the "wee wee" goes in the chair.

Chapter 4 - How to Stop Stressing

Relax. Keep your sense of humor. When your child senses your stress they'll be upset, too. This only makes the process harder for both of you. It easier said than done, but remember that every parent has been through this phase. They survived and so will you and your child.

Don't expect your child to master potty training in a few days and then you won't be disappointed.

Stop listening to the advice of mother in laws, friends, and other mothers. It doesn't matter when their children were potty trained.

Enlist the help of your spouse if at all possible. You and your child will both need a break from each other on occasion. If the other parent can step in it will help relieve stress for all of you. But make sure you're using the same methods and rewards.

Try to find the fun in this adventure. This will be easier some days than others.

Chapter 5 - Getting Started

If you've started your preparation, then you are already watching your child for signs of when they need to go to the bathroom.

There are several steps your child will have to learn to be potty trained.

Realizing when they need to urinate or have a bowel movement. It will take awhile for them to fully understand this sensation.

Getting to the bathroom and pulling their pants and underwear down.

Sitting on the potty long enough to "wee wee" or "poop".

Wiping themselves clean with toilet paper. You might want to teach them to use six blocks of toilet paper or a length that reaches to the floor. Otherwise, they seem to get carried away and use huge stacks of toilet paper. This is a mess in the potty chair and can make the "real" toilet clog.

Washing their hands when they're done. Teach them to use soap and wash their hands. You'll probably need a small stool that they can stand on to reach the faucet, soap, and a towel on their own.

This all seems easy for an adult. But this is long list of tasks for a toddler. Don't expect them to remember everything immediately. You'll need to remind them to clean up and wash their hands.

You can start letting your child sit on the potty chair fully clothed for a few times to get use to idea of sitting. Let them look at a book or read a book to them.

Talk to your child's day care or preschool and let them know when you're going to start potty training. You'll need them to be on board with your plan. Find out what they require from you and what they are willing to do to help. Let them know your child's schedule as much as possible.

Chapter 6 - Day One of Potty Training

On day one of potty training you should plan to stay home most of the day. When possible, try to start training in the warmer months of the year. It's not very enticing for a child to start pulling down their pants and sitting on a cold potty chair. If it is winter then try to keep the house a little warmer than usual until your child gets use to sitting on the potty.

Have the potty chair and rewards ready in the bathroom. Your child should already be comfortable with the chair and even use to sitting on it.

Dress your child in clothes that are easy for them to pull down such as loose shorts or pants. This isn't the day for overalls or pants with buttons.

Feed your child breakfast as normal while he or she is still wearing a diaper.

After breakfast immediately dress them in their big kid underwear and take them to sit on their potty chair. Read a book while they sit there. Reward them for sitting there even if nothing happens.

If you've been tracking your child's wet diaper times then you'll have some clue as to when to take them back to the potty.

When they actually go on the potty make a big deal about it. Give them TWO stickers or two M&M's or raisins. One for going and sitting on the potty and one for going "wee wee" in the potty.

Show them how to wipe with toilet paper. You'll probably have to help your child with this for awhile, especially after bowel movements.

Teach them to wash their hands every time they leave the bathroom. You can give them a sticker or a star for remembering to wash their hands.

You might want to offer a big incentive at the end of the day. A special game the child enjoys, the child's favorite dinner or dessert, or a favorite DVD. Make sure everyone in the family participates in this big "end of the first potty day" event. It should be a huge deal and make the child feel special. Celebrate the day even if the child only had a few actual successes. The point is to celebrate the fact that sat on the potty at the times you asked them to.

When your child tells you he needs to go potty take them immediately. Get off the phone, put down your book, turn off the vacuum, and get them to the bathroom. At first they won't realize very far in advance when they need to go; so you need to be available to take them quickly.

Many children need to sit on the potty right after they finish lunch and dinner. Don't worry about clearing the table or doing the dishes. Help them sit on the potty for at least a few minutes. If nothing happens then you'll need to try again in 30 minutes.

This is especially important during the first few days of training. That's one reason it's important not to plan a lot of other activities for the first day or two. Don't try to do your spring cleaning on the day you start potty training your child. Though this seems obvious, as a parent you know how busy you are and how often you're multitasking. But this is one time when it's important to focus on helping your child achieve this important milestone. Let the house cleaning go for a day or two.

Chapter 7 - Potty Training for Boys

It's usually easier for boys to learn potty training by sitting down. This helps avoid confusion between urinating and having a bowel movement. It's easy for them to get confused about whether this is a "sit down" or "stand up" moment.

Plus, it's a lot less messy if they learn sitting down. Their aim will not be good in the beginning so sitting down helps avoid this problem.

You might want to use a deflector on your son's potty chair. You'll need to show him how to carefully sit down to keep from hurting himself on the deflector, though. If he gets hurt he won't want to sit on the chair again.

If you don't use a deflector you'll probably need to teach your son to point his penis down while he urinates.

As he gets a little older and understands the difference between urinating and bowel movements; then you'll want to teach him to stand up while urinating. Some parents have found that putting something like Cheerios or other cereal in the toilet and letting their son "aim" for it helps them to learn accuracy and cuts down on messes.

Let your son watch his daddy go to the bathroom so he can understand the concept of standing up to urinate.

Chapter 8 - Potty Training for Girls

Generally, girls are a little easier to potty train than boys. They are also usually ready earlier.

There are many reasons suspected for their earlier ability to potty train. One reason is they're usually more verbal and able to communicate better sooner than boys.

Also, it can be easier for girls to sit on the potty and not have to worry about pointing a penis down.

If you have an older daughter then don't expect your younger son to be trained at the same time your daughter was. He will probably be ready at a later time.

But there are always exceptions to every statistic. The main thing to remember with siblings is that they are individuals and they'll be ready on their own schedule. This is even true with twins. Even though they are the same age and are being trained with exactly the same methods; one might be ready and successful sooner than the other. Don't make the child feel guilty because they are not training as quickly as their sibling.

Chapter 9 - Books and DVDs Can Help

Letting your child read picture books and watch videos about potty training can be a big boost to your efforts. First off, they'll enjoy looking at the books while they're sitting on the potty which makes them willing to sit longer. Have a few books that they can only read while sitting on their chair.

When looking at potty training books they'll see pictures of other children their size using the toilet. This helps them know this is a common thing that other kids do; not some crazy scheme that only their parents thought of on their own.

By reading books to them about potty training you're helping to reinforce the idea in their young mind. It helps them understand how the whole concept works.

Watching DVDs and seeing other children their age using the potty helps, too. It teaches them that "this is what the big kids do".

There are a multitude of adorable picture books about potty training that you can find online and at local bookstores. Your child will enjoy having you read these books to them and they'll also get a better idea of the whole process. It's a good idea to look through the books and find the ones that best match the method of potty training your using. Some will show a child using a potty chair and other will have them using a regular sized toilet. Pick books that match the choices you've made to train your child.

Chapter 10 - Tricks and Games to Make Potty Training More Fun

Using a reward system can make potty training more fun for your child and therefore easier for you. Some parents say they don't want to use "bribery" to potty train their child. But this is just positive reinforcement.

Here are a few suggestions for prizes:

-Stickers

-Fish crackers

-Small pieces of candy

-Raisins

-Tattoos

-Small stuffed animals

-Glow sticks

You might want to consider buying a small cardboard treasure chest and filling it with prizes. Then your child gets to pick a prize each time he's successful on the potty. These can be purchased cheaply online. Make sure the prizes are age appropriate and don't pose a choking threat.

Put a poster or a calendar on the wall. Give your child a star every time they go potty.

You can also add a sticker if they remember to wash their hands on their own. If you don't want to give them a prize each time, you could give them a prize every time they get five stickers on the poster.

Once your child has gone a whole day without accidents you can present them with a trophy or a bigger toy as a prize.

You can give them a certificate to put on the wall that shows they've completed one full week or month of potty training.

Some parents like to throw a party after the child has had a successful week of training.

You might not feel comfortable rewarding your child with prizes for potty training. This is your choice to make. But make the decision in advance. Don't start training offering rewards and then change your mind after a few days.

Choose which method of rewards you're going to use and be consistent.

The most important reward you can give your child is your praise. Let them know how proud you are of them and the progress they are making. Don't let yourself get distracted and not really pay attention when they have good day.

Chapter 11 - 7 Things to Never Do When You are Potty Training Your Child

1. Start too early. You'll only stress yourself and your child if you start before they are ready physically and emotionally. If they can't feel and understand when they're about to urinate then they can't tell you.

2. Refuse to admit you started too early. If you realize your child is not ready; then stop for now and try again in a few weeks or months.

3. Listen to the advice of too many people. You'll receive tons of suggestions on how they did it and why you should do it exactly the same way. You know your child better than anyone else so you're ultimately responsible for the timing and methods you choose. Don't let anyone guilt trip you into doing anything you or child are not comfortable with.

4. Let yourself stress out to much. Potty training is hard. But when you stress you make a tough situation even harder.

5. Be disappointed when your child isn't potty trained within a day or two.

6. Scold your child or spank them when they have accidents. This will only upset them and they'll want nothing to do with the whole "potty training" thing. Offer positive reinforcement but don't be negative when things don't go as planned. Don't use words like "yucky" or "stinky" when your child has an accident.

7. Not making the training fun and positive. Potty training will always have stressful moments, but you can do your best to add fun and reward your child when they are successful.

Chapter 12 - Overnight Potty Training

Even after your child has mastered day time potty training; it may still take awhile before they can go all night without an accident.

This is usually just the result of a heavy sleeper who doesn't wake up to feel the sensation of needing to go potty.

You can let your child wear pull up type diapers during the night for awhile if you prefer.

Don't let your child drink anything right before going to bed. Try to stop their fluid intake at least an hour before bedtime.

Always let them sit on the potty right before going to bed.

Keep extra bedding, pajamas, and underwear handy so if they have to change during the night you won't have to search through drawers to find what you need.

Use a plastic mattress cover to protect the bed.

Teach your child to practice stopping and starting urinating in the potty. This helps to strengthen the muscles that control them relieving their bladder. When they get up in the night they'll have better control and therefore a better chance of getting to the bathroom in time.

You might need to wake your child up during the night to go to the bathroom if they still aren't successful after several months of training.

If bed wetting continues after several months you should talk to your pediatrician to help eliminate any fears of any physical problems.

If your child is still wetting the bed when they are over five years old you might want to consider using an alarm system. These will wake your child as soon as they start to empty their bladder. There are several types of bed wetting alarms that you can purchase online. Some of the systems have dual alarms so one will sound in your room as well as the child's. This means you can make sure your child wakes up and gets to the bathroom in time. But you won't have to sleep in the same room with them to hear the alarm.

Never scold or get angry at your child for wetting the bed.

Don't let siblings tease the child about bed wetting.

Chapter 13 - What to Do When You Travel

Sometimes a child will master potty training at home but still have problems when they go out. You can help this problem by making sure your child doesn't drink anything shortly before you leave the house. Be sure they go to the bathroom right before you leave.

When you get to a store ask your child if they need to go to the bathroom. Familiarize yourself with the location of the bathrooms at all the stores you use regularly. That way when you have to make a quick trip you'll at least know where you're going. Never shop more than 30 – 45 minutes without asking your child if they need to go to use the bathroom.

It can be a little tricky when a father is out with his daughter. Most dads aren't comfortable taking their daughter into the men's restroom. Luckily, a lot of stores now have a family bathroom. This makes it much easier for a mom with her son or a dad with his toddler daughter to take them to the potty. Never let your toddler go into a restroom alone.

Traveling over night: One of things that helps a child with their potty training is having a set schedule. Being in a new place with a mixed up schedule can result in their having accidents again.

If at all possible, try to start your potty training at a time when you're not planning to travel or take a vacation away from home for the first month or two. When that's not possible then you'll have to adjust your traveling to include potty training time.

Consider using pull-up type pants while you're traveling. It might set your potty training back a little but it may be worth it to avoid the stress. You might at least take some with you in case you need to use them at some point during the trip.

When you're driving for long periods of time you're going to have to stop often. This can seem frustrating but it must be done. Don't expect your child to be able to go for hours without a potty break. Plus, it's hard for a toddler to travel for long in the car at the best of times. When you stop at a rest stop make sure you give your child time to run around and use some energy. The good news is, your back will feel better because you took the time to stop and you won't get as sleepy.

Things you should take with you when you travel:

Portable potty chair – make sure your child has used this potty chair and is already familiar with it. If you can't find a public restroom at the right time you'll have their chair handy. They'll also be more comfortable using their own chair than the one at a new house or a hotel.

Wet wipes – You can never have too many of these when you travel. They are not only for cleaning up after the child goes to the bathroom; but also they can be used after eating sticky snacks.

Extra clothes and underwear – Always have several sets of extra clothes handy in a bag in the car. You don't want to have to unpack the trunk and search through suitcases to find a fresh set of clothes if your child has a accident.

Don't give your child constant drinks while you're driving. Don't let them get too thirsty or dehydrated, of course, but they don't need to be drinking all the time. This will just make them have to go the bathroom more often.

Chapter 14 – Possible Problems

Most children become potty training without any major issues. It may seem stressful to you and them while you're going through it; but when it's over you'll think, "that wasn't so bad".

Don't worry if your child has a good week and then has an accident. Sometimes they are simply too busy playing to want to take the time to go potty. This is normal. You'll experience good days of training and days of set- backs. Just carry on and know that eventually there will be fewer and fewer accidents.

If your child becomes constipated during potty training you should talk to your pediatrician. He can give you recommendations on how to handle this situation. Make sure your child is drinking plenty of water. The pediatrician might also suggest a change in diet to make sure they child's stool is not too hard. Passing a hard stool can be painful and therefore make the child resist having a bowel movement.

Some strong-willed children have a problem with potty training. The best thing to do is just continue and find out what motivates them to go to the potty. Some children are thrilled to get a few goldfish as a reward, others want stickers, and some just want you to sit with them and read them a book.

Conclusion

Potty training is a big step in you and your child's life. It is one of the first milestones. Make sure you let them know how proud you are of them. Make it a big deal.

But remember not to stress too much on the way there. Keep your sense of humor along the way.

When you get discouraged, remember how much money you're going to saving on diapers when this is all over.

Try to make the process as positive and fun for your child as possible. Reward and praise them often.

Made in United States
North Haven, CT
24 February 2022

16440217R00028